PRACTICAL TATTING

PRACTICAL TATTING

Phyllis Sparks

B.T. Batsford Ltd · London

ACKNOWLEDGEMENTS

I am very grateful to my brother and sister-in-law, James and Wendy Adam, for taking the photographs with such infinite care. Wendy also arranged the lace and provided the elegant props, which made the pictures so much more attractive.

My thanks go, too, to my son Peter for a lot of practical help, and a little gentle bullying when I got despondent or just plain lazy.

Phyllis Sparks

First published 1994

© Phyllis Sparks 1994

Cover photography: Trevor Hurst

Typeset by Saxon Graphics Ltd, Derby
and printed in Great Britain by Butler & Tanner Ltd, Frome

Published by
B.T. Batsford Ltd
4 Fitzhardinge Street
London W1H 0AH

A catalogue record for this book is available from the British Library

ISBN 0 7134 6346 5

CONTENTS

PREFACE

'There are enough books teaching people how to tat,' I proclaimed. 'Every book you see starts off with drawings of hands and shuttles making the knot. People don't need telling again. And besides, I can't draw. I want to go on from there ... invent new patterns, be a bit adventurous ... see what I can do.'

'All right,' said my publisher, 'an advanced book on tatting.'

This pulled me up a bit. What qualifications have I to write an advanced book on tatting? Other people take exams and diplomas, but I taught myself, many years ago, from the instructions at the beginning of a pattern book. Then I lapsed – there was a house to clean, babies to look after, children's clothes to make.

Then, a few years ago, I took it up again. I found that there were no new pattern books available, although several were in the process of being published. So I made up a few little edgings and one or two rather aimless circles. Then I got braver and made first one collar, then another. People liked them. 'You ought to write a book,' they said.

Terrified of making a public idiot of myself (I had never had a tatting lesson in my life and might be doing it all wrong for all I knew), I decided to go back to the beginning. I took a week's course at the English Lace School at Rockbeare (now sadly defunct) with Marjorie Brooking, who *does* know what she is talking about. 'It would be better if you pulled the threads tighter,' she said, 'and you could do it quicker if you held the shuttle *this* way.' Reassured, I persevered.

So we dropped 'Advanced' from the title of this book and put in 'Practical' instead. If you want to learn the different techniques used in tatting – making twisted chains, incorporating beads, and all the clever stuff – I would recommend Rebecca Jones's *The Complete Book of Tatting*, which could probably be described as the definitive book on the subject, and will give you all the inspiration and practical advice you'll need.

We are all different, and there is room for all of us. I wouldn't, personally, wear tatted, beaded ear-rings to save my life. My granddaughters would be embarrassed. I have therefore compiled a straightforward, practical book of edgings, collars and insertions, containing, I hope, original and appealing designs, and including a few patterns just for fun. Who's writing this book, anyway?

THE DIAGRAMS

All the tatters I have talked to agree that it is easier to work a pattern from a diagram than from any other form of instruction. This, as you can imagine, presents problems for a person like me who cannot draw. I get by with a ruler, an old geometry set, and two templates bought from a technical-drawing shop. One of them has a series of about twenty-five ovals with diameters varying from approximately 2 mm. to 3 cm.; the other has a similar variety of circles. They have marks at north, south, east and west, which enable you to keep them in a straight line.

I start by drawing a grid of 1 cm. squares, using fairly heavy ink, so that the lines can be seen through a piece of ordinary typing paper. I then draw the diagonals in both directions. In this way I can draw any straight-line pattern, such as the edging shown in fig a:

For the circular patterns, draw a number of concentric circles, again about a centimetre apart. If the pattern you want to draw starts with five rings, divide the circle into five and draw five radii from the centre of the circle, i.e. each 72° apart. Then line up your chosen oval, with the north–south axis along a radius, and the east–west along a suitable circle (see fig. b). Join these rings with one of the circles on your template, and mark the picots on the semi-circles by eye. It should not be necessary to measure these. If you then draw the ovals for the next round of the pattern opposite these marks, with the east–west axis on the template aligned with one of the concentric circles, they should be in the right position.

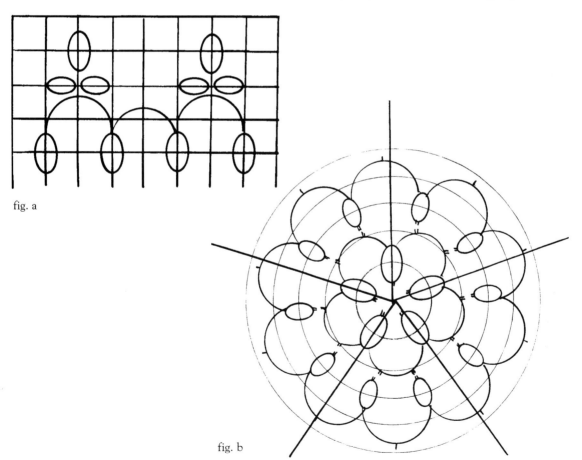

fig. a

fig. b

SYMBOLS USED IN THIS BOOK

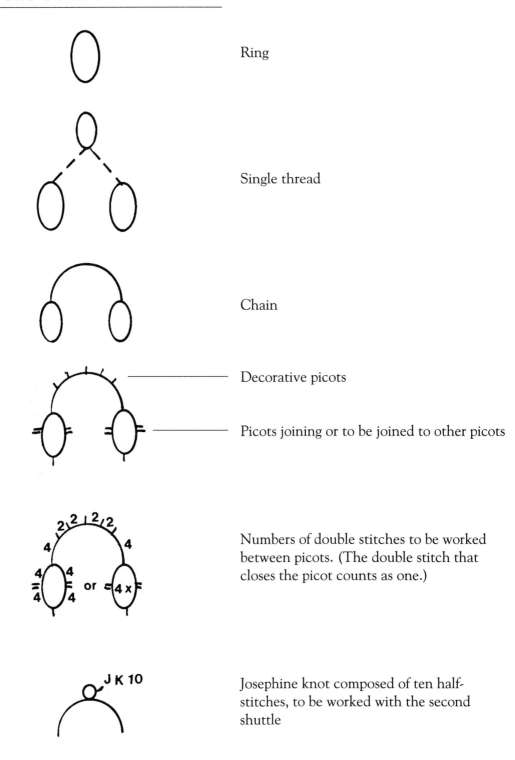

Ring

Single thread

Chain

Decorative picots

Picots joining or to be joined to other picots

Numbers of double stitches to be worked between picots. (The double stitch that closes the picot counts as one.)

Josephine knot composed of ten half-stitches, to be worked with the second shuttle

FOUR SIMPLE
HANDKERCHIEF
EDGINGS

EDGING A

I used no. 50 DMC Cordonnet Special cotton for this edging. The finer the thread used, of course, the more delicate the edging will be. I once made a version of this design in 100 Cordonnet Special for a handkerchief, and it won the non-bobbin section at a lace day in Penzance.

The first row needs only a shuttle thread, but in the second row the ball thread should be wound on to a second shuttle, as it will be needed for working the 5 ds p 5 ds ring which joins it to the first row. Try to get the single thread joining the rings in the first row an even 3 mm. in length – it is obvious from the photograph that I didn't do so at the corner!

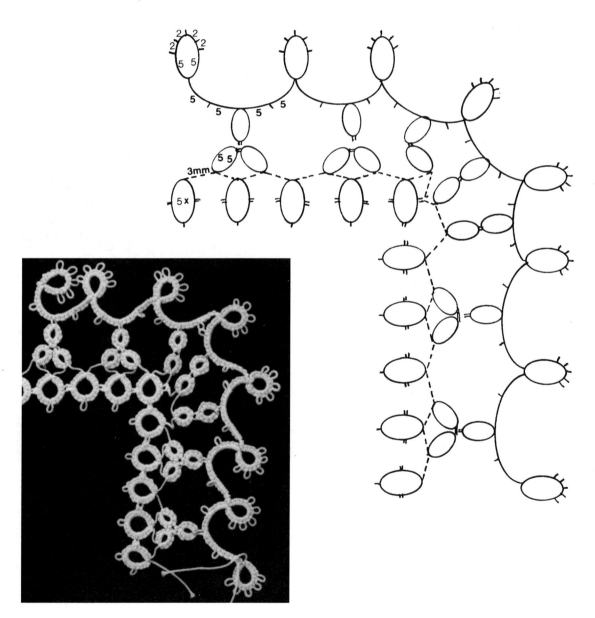

EDGING B

This is a very simple little edging which, if you like the instructions written out, goes like this:

Ring 3 ds p three times, 9 ds

Chain 2 ds p seven times, 2 ds. Join with shuttle thread to third p on ring, and repeat.

At the corner, after joining the chain to the 3rd p of the ring, make another chain, then a ring of 9 ds, join to the second p of previous ring, 3 ds p twice and 3 ds. Then make the ring of 3 ds p three times 9 ds, and the chain as before. Do not forget to join the first p of each chain to the last p of the previous chain, otherwise it tends to twist up.

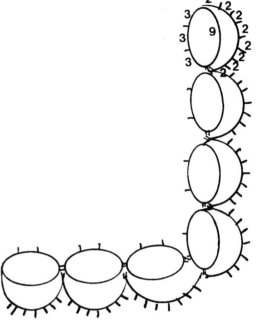

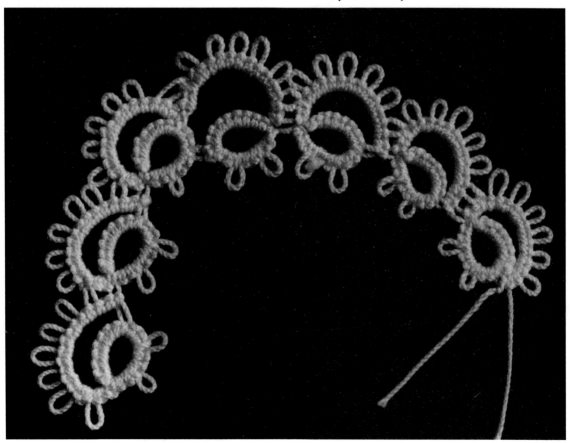

EDGING C

This pattern is worked in two rows. It does
not really matter which you do first, but it is
probably easier to measure if you start with
the footside. I really cannot see any
difficulties to point out, so I leave it to you!

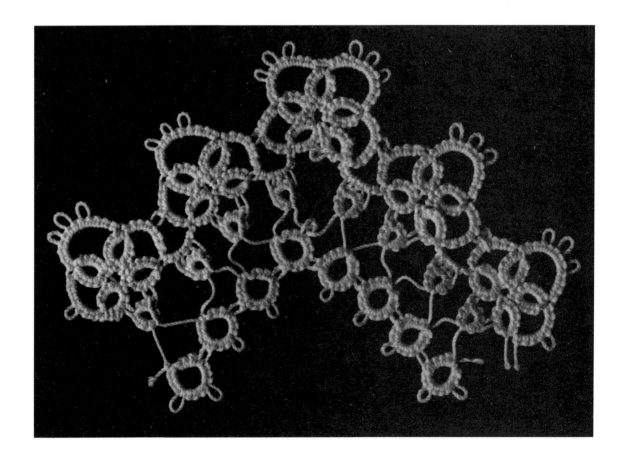

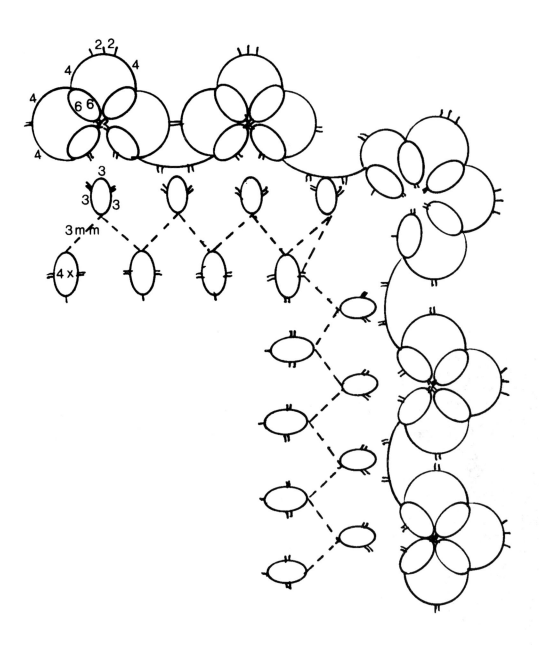

EDGING D

This pattern is much simpler than it looks. You will need to wind the ball thread on to a second shuttle, which is used to work the Josephine knots. These are made by working the first half of the stitch only, in this case ten times, and pulling the thread through in the same way as for an ordinary ring. It's a bit fiddly to do as ten half-stitches make a very small circle and the shuttle thread tends to twist itself up and is difficult to pull through. Pay no attention to the large size of the cross-over circle at the corner of the diagram. The diagram has been opened out to make it easier to read, and these anomalies sometimes happen.

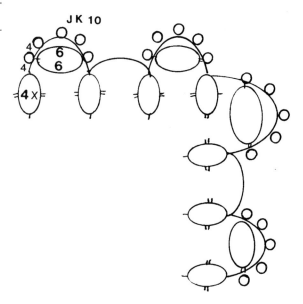

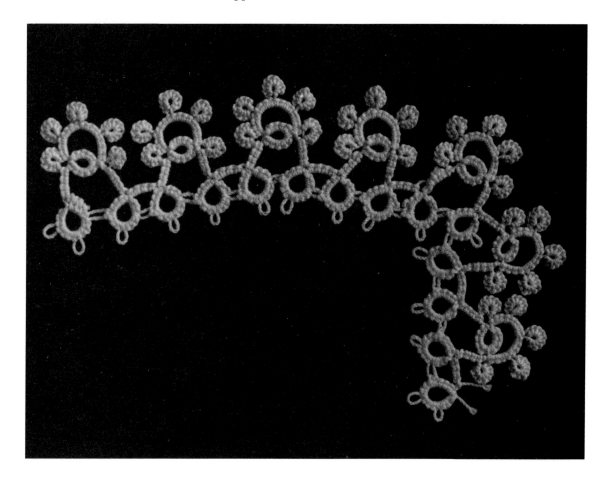

EDGINGS
FOR
GARMENTS

TEA-TIME PINAFORE

This looks complicated; the problem, of
course, is to make the fern bend over the
flower. If you are careful to follow the
joining-up picots, you should not have any
problems. Work the footing first. You need
six repeats to complete each pattern. Do
not cut the thread after winding it on to the
shuttle from the ball – just hook it through
the picot to begin the fern.

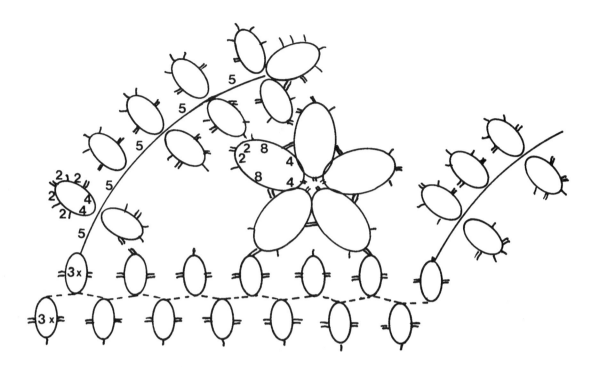

TWO WAIST SLIPS

Slip 1: Edging

I think this one is fairly clear. You will need
to wind the ball thread on to a second
shuttle to work the rings in the first and
third rows. The large circle in the middle of
the flower is worked as a chain and closed at
the picot. There are some unavoidable
distortions in the diagram, which has been
opened out for clarification, but if you keep
an eye on the photograph, you should not
have any trouble. Worked in no. 40 DMC
Cordonnet Special, the edging is about
3.5 cm. (1½ in.) wide, and this should be
taken into account if you are using a
shop-bought petticoat.

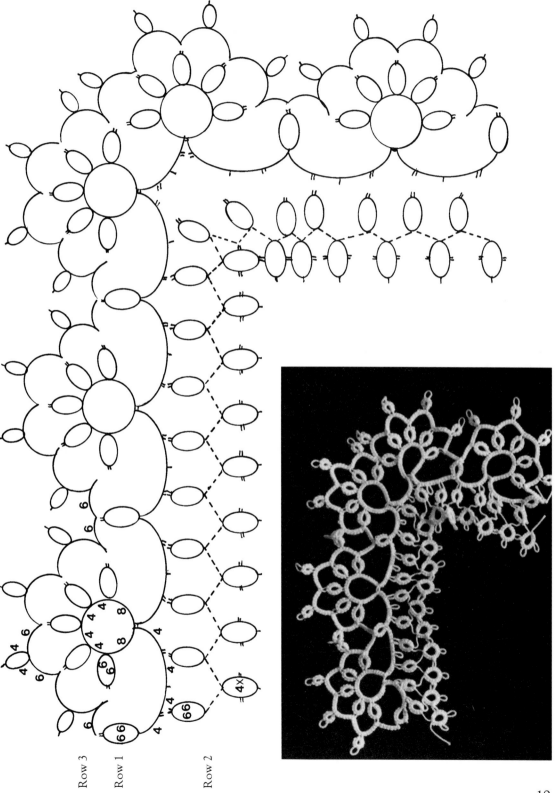

Row 3

Row 1

Row 2

Slip 2: Edging

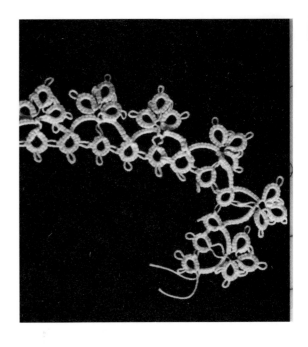

This pattern is not quite so simple as it looks. Work with the usual no. 40 or 50 DMC Cordonnet Special thread, and wind the ball thread on to a second shuttle.

First shuttle R. 4 ds p three times, 4 ds. Ch. 10 ds.

Second shuttle Work the trefoil as shown on the diagram.

First shuttle Make a locking stitch, i.e. work the second half of the ds 'wrong' (with the shuttle thread wound round the ball thread) to prevent it slipping. Leave a gap of about 5 mm. (¼ in.) of thread, and work the 4 ds p three times, 4 ds ring. Leave another 5 mm. thread, and make another locking stitch before continuing the 10 ds chain.

The tricky bit is getting the two locking stitches close enough together, and the two 5 mm. threads exactly the same length.

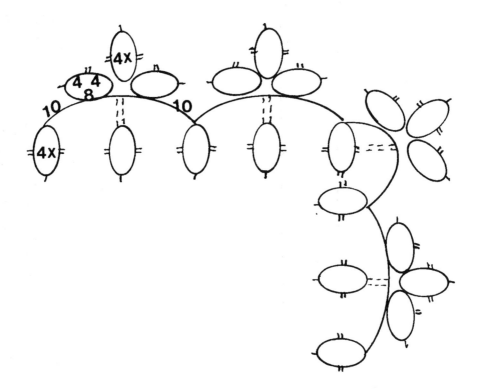

Slip 2: Insertion

In order for this insertion to lie flat you have to vary the length of the threads leading from the rings. Those leading to the central ring of the 'flower' should be shortest, and the others slightly longer.

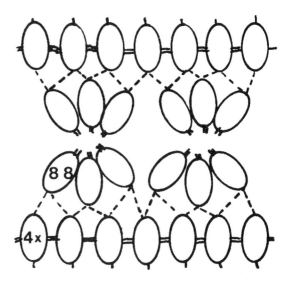

I have no doubt you can buy a pattern for these slips but, unless you have an overlocking machine, it is difficult not to make the seams lumpy. I'm afraid I cheated and bought them – they had awful machine lace and were not expensive. I cut a few inches off the bottom of this one, and made the frill out of fine poly-cotton. I oversewed the raw edges by hand, pressed about 5 mm. to the inside, and oversewed the tatting to the folded edge. It stayed in position without needing a visible hem.

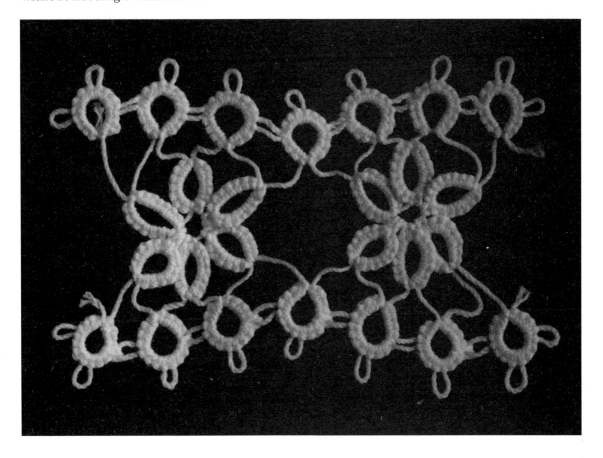

EDGING A

I made this little dress purely as an example for this book, out of a man's pale-blue shirt which I bought at a jumble sale for 20p. It shows how effective a really simple pattern can be. Use a fairly fine thread (50 DMC Cordonnet Special, for instance). The chain on the outside is too long, but will lie flat after ironing.

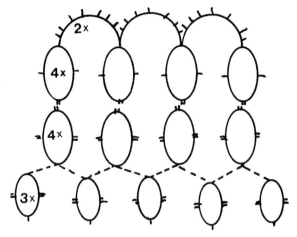

May I put in a plea here for smocking? It is so simple to do, and yet looks very effective. Full instructions can be found in *The Batsford Encyclopedia of Embroidery Techniques* (see 'Further Reading', p. 92). I don't know why smocking is thought to be difficult. It is a little tedious, perhaps, picking up all those spots, but if you have the patience for tatting you can surely manage smocking!

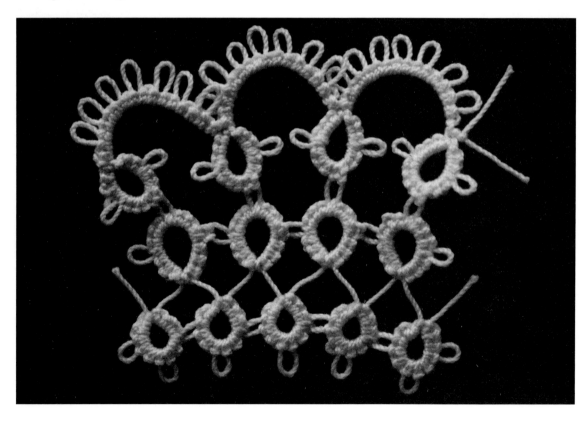

EDGING B

I see this child's pinafore worn over a dark-coloured, long-sleeved party dress, which would probably be made of velvet, or something equally unwashable, so the pinny would be practical as well as pretty. I made it out of poly-cotton from a sun-dress pattern, altered to button at the back. The tatting looks complicated, but it is very simple, really. If you use the photograph as well as the diagram, it should not present any problems. You need only one shuttle and ball thread for the first three rows, but should wind the ball thread on to a second shuttle for the fourth row, to work the small rings on the outside edge. I suggest size 40 or 50 DMC Cordonnet Special thread.

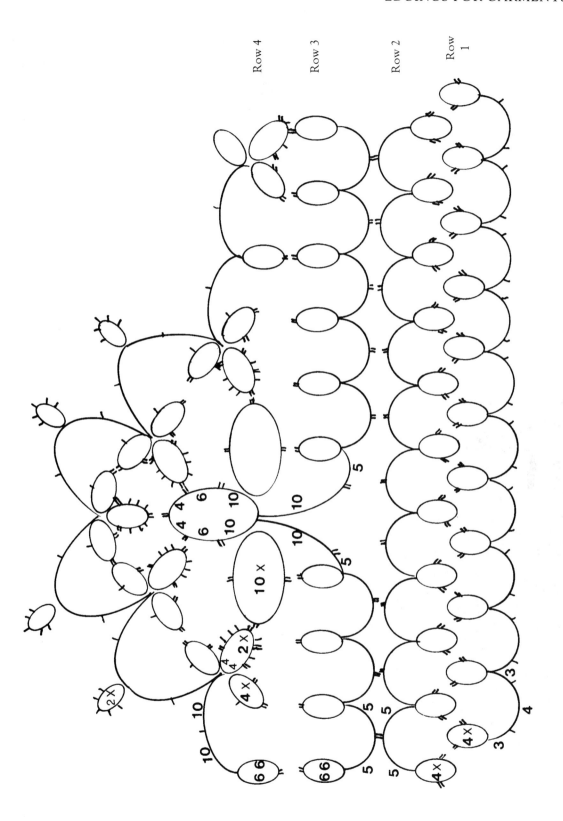

Row 4

Row 3

Row 2

Row 1

EDGING C

This is another very simple little edging, which is made using no. 40 or 50 DMC Cordonnet Special thread.

I have included a corner so that the edging can be used for a handkerchief as well. (A finer thread will be required, of course.) A variation with a picot on the chain, i.e. 3 ds p 3 ds on either side of the Josephine knot, is also possible, and is a little less austere.

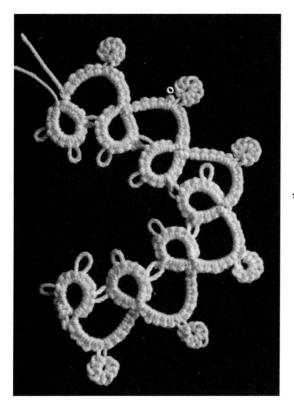

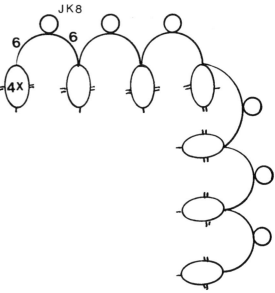

THREE
COLLARS

COLLAR A

This pattern looks complicated, but the actual tatting is simple enough. With the ball thread wound on to a second shuttle (for working the small rings in the middle), start with ring A and work along the row, allowing three rings to a pattern, until the collar is big enough. Now work one more ring, then the end section, and return along the other side, joining the little rings to the first half. Complete the end section, working back to ring A.

Start row 2 along the footing (neck) edge, then work up the front edge of the collar, linking with the middle section as shown, along the zigzag outer-edge section, and working down the other front edge. Sew off into the small ring of the footing.

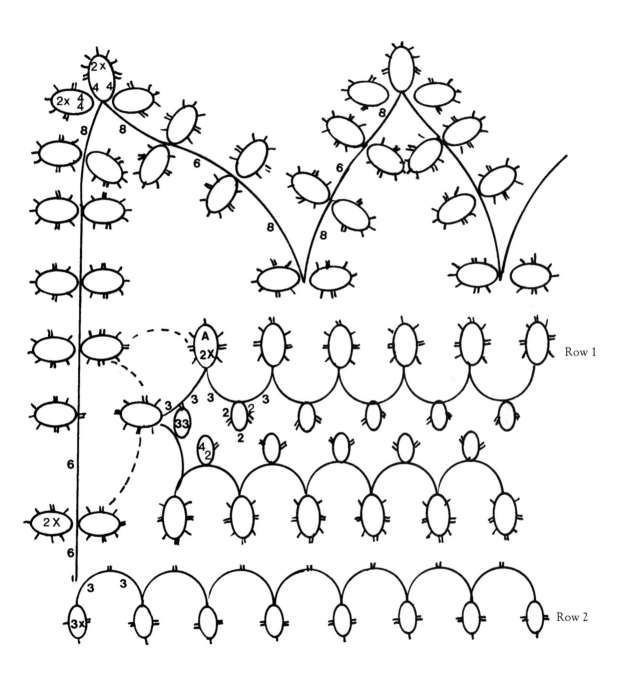

Row 1

Row 2

COLLAR B

This pattern is quite straightforward to work. The lozenge-shaped section is made with the thread wound on two shuttles, the ball-thread shuttle being used to work the four inside rings. The two halves of the stalk section should be joined together at the base of the leaves by hooking the shuttle thread through the base of the opposite leaf, after working each leaf and before continuing the stem chain. The flower starts with a ring of 12 p separated by 2 ds. The second row is worked with one shuttle only and a space of about 3 mm. or ¼ in. between rings; the footing pulls it together into a nice curve.

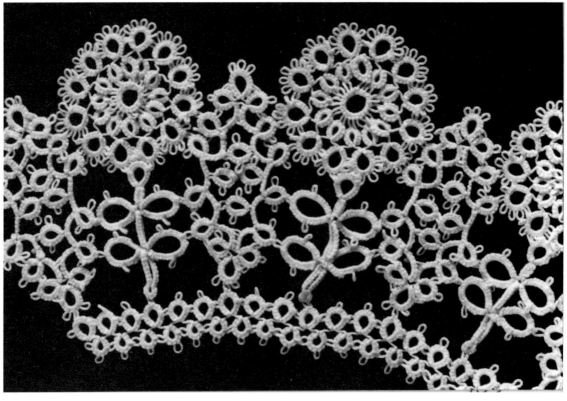

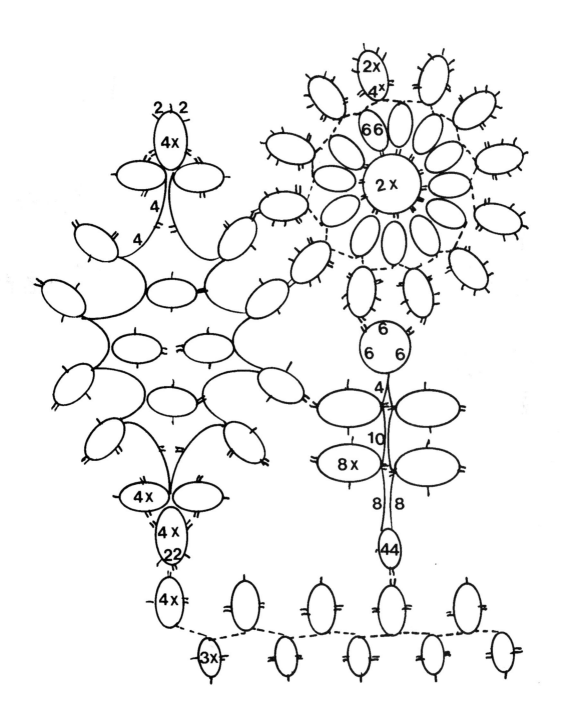

COLLAR C

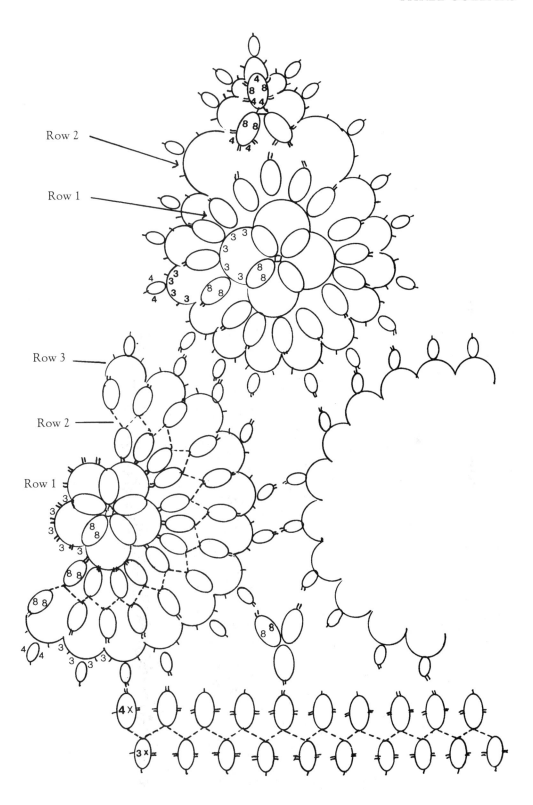

Row 2

Row 1

Row 3

Row 2

Row 1

You will find this collar easier if you make
the circles first, joining them to one another
where appropriate with the little (4 ds p 4
ds) rings (worked with the second shuttle) in
row 3. Next, work the small stabilising
group of three (8 ds p 8 ds) rings, followed
by the footing. Finally add the pointed oval
shape. Row 1 of this shape is worked with
two shuttles, the first for the four central
rings and the chain, and the second for the
outer (8 ds p 8 ds) rings. The oval shape is
made with the three rings at the pointed end
(note they are not all the same size). The
outer row (row 2) is the same as the third
row of the big circles, and is repeated all the
way round, in spite of the differences that
appear on the diagram.

THREE
MATS

MAT A

This little mat has a rather chequered history. I started making it many years ago, and then lost interest in the middle of the third round. When I found it again, the instructions were long gone, so the rest of it is my own unaided work! Will whoever invented rows one, two and three please forgive me?

The working is extremely simple, requiring only one shuttle and ball thread throughout. I made it in no. 40 crochet cotton.

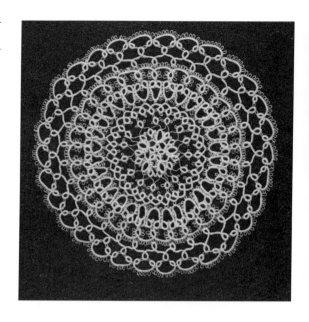

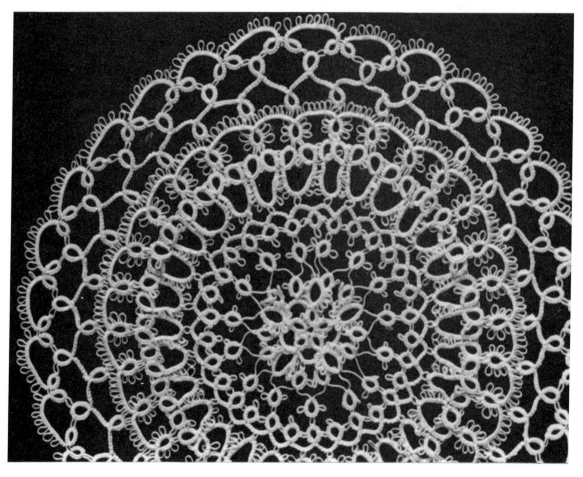

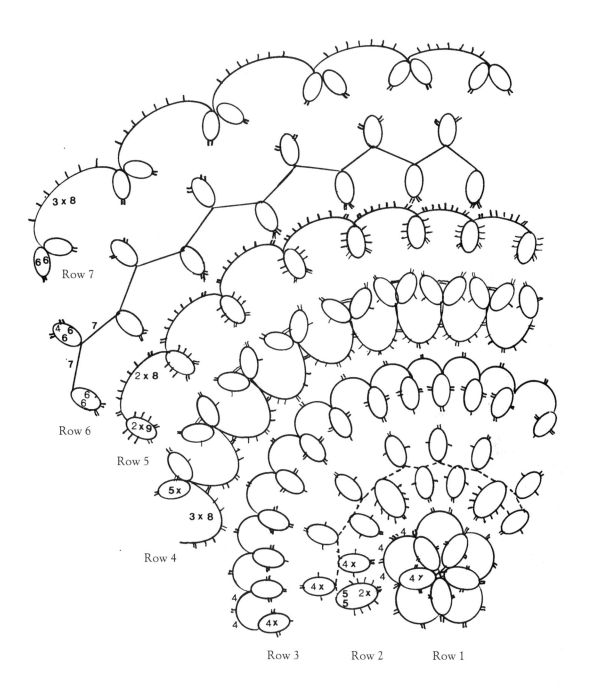

3 x 8

6 6   Row 7

4 6
6   7

7

6
6   Row 6

2 x 8

2 x 9   Row 5

5 x

3 x 8

Row 4

4 x

4   4 x

4

Row 3   Row 2   Row 1

4

4 x

5 2 x
5

4 y

MAT B

This mat has a basic square motif, repeated to make the central square (in no. 40 cotton for a small mat, and no. 20 for a tablecloth). The basic square is worked all in one row, with the ball thread wound on to a second shuttle to work the eight outside rings. The first row of the border is worked with one shuttle and a ball thread, but the second, third and fourth rows all have the ball thread wound on to a second shuttle. This second shuttle is used in the second row for the two (6 ds p 6 ds) rings outside the chain. The third row is worked in the same way (NB at the corners there are four chains with only one ring each, forming the little groups of four rings). In the fourth row the second shuttle is used to make the groups of three rings and, of course, the Josephine knots. The fourth row seems to go round the corner quite happily without alteration.

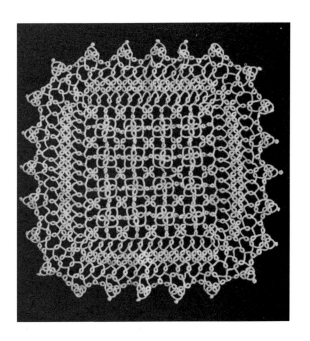

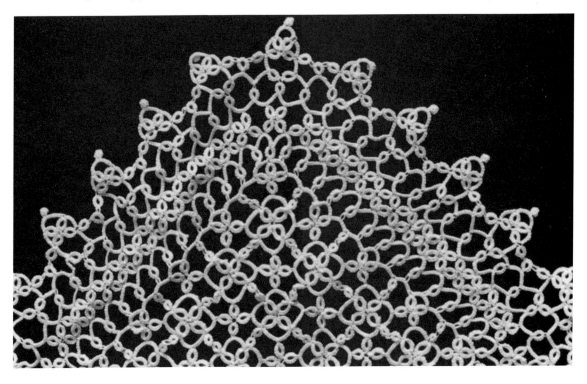

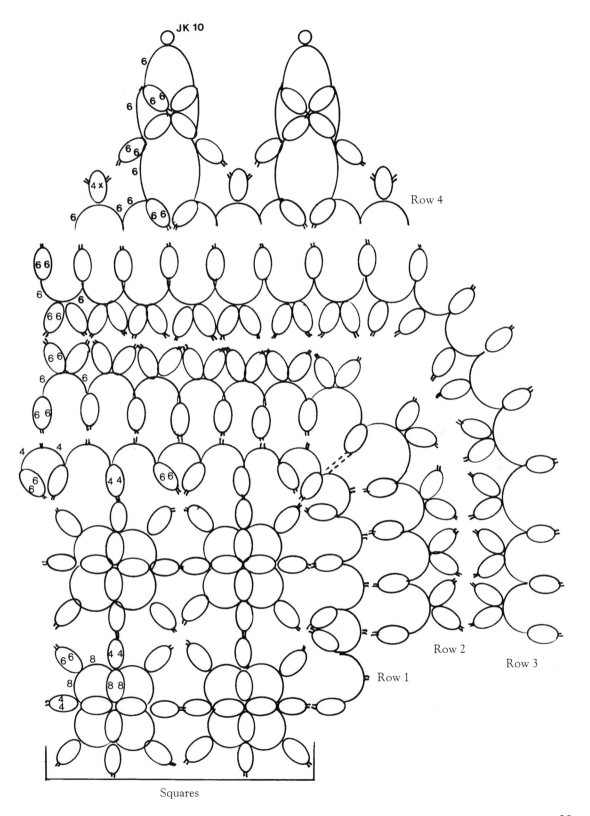

JK 10

Row 4

Row 2

Row 3

Row 1

Squares

MAT C

The nice thing about building up a mat from a single repeated motif is the way it makes secondary patterns on its own. On the other hand, the constant repetitions are tedious to work. If you are one of those people whose fingers can work automatically, and who can keep on tatting while reading a book or watching television, you could use this pattern to make a splendid tablecloth in no. 20 thread without getting bored. But if, like me, you get bored easily, just make a little mat with a finer cotton.

There are only two rows. The first is a ring of 3 ds p, worked six times. The second, which needs the ball thread wound on to a second shuttle to work the 12 outer rings, is nearly as simple.

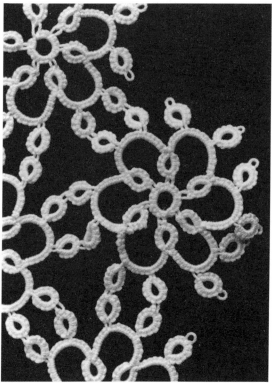

EDGINGS FOR HOUSEHOLD LINEN

TABLE MAT

I hope the diagram for this pattern makes the working method clear. The large centre circle of the flower is worked as a chain and closed into a ring by the picot. In this way the petals can be worked as rings with the second shuttle, as you come to them.

Ideally, you should make six of these mats for an impressive dinner-party setting. They should be made of linen and hemstitched by hand, with mitred corners.

There is a lot of work involved, and linen costs a fortune, but the satisfaction when you have finished will make it all worthwhile. The hemstitching, mitreing, etc. is all explained in *The Batsford Encyclopedia of Embroidery Techniques* (see 'Further Reading', p. 92). I did mine in no. 40 DMC Cordonnet Special. It would be a terrible waste of time and effort to make the edging and then sew it on to inferior material.

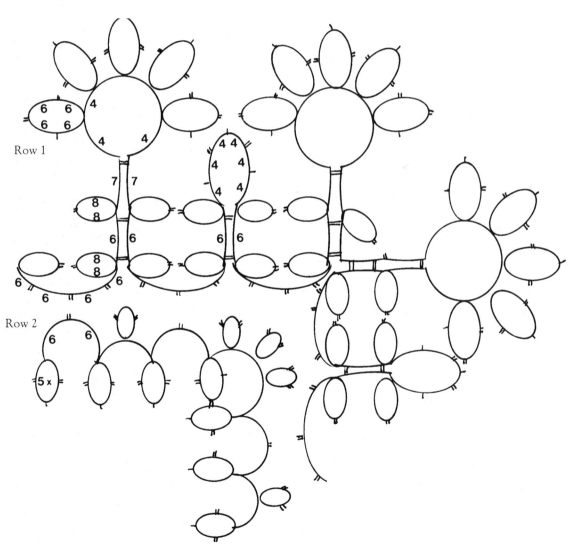

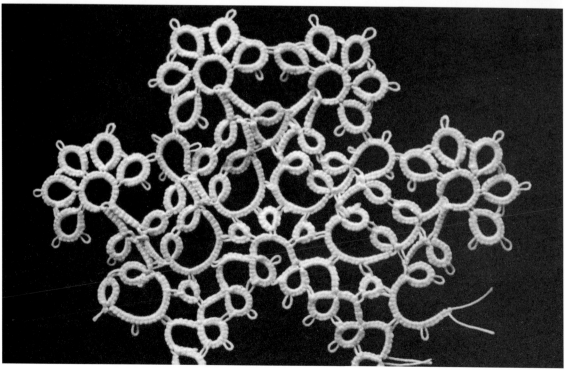

MATS FOR A DRESSING-TABLE

After the chain at the base, leave a fairly
large picot and work a 5 ds chain. Next,
work the ring for the 'petal', then another 5
ds chain; join to the large picot and repeat
for the five petals. These mats are oval
shaped and do not need a corner, but I have
designed one anyway, in case you want to
use it for other things. I actually bought
these mats at a jumble sale, and they
originally had some rather nasty coarse lace,
which I took off. I then trimmed the ragged
edges and rolled them (as described in
Mounting and Using Lace by Jean Withers,
see p. 92), so that they looked reasonably
presentable.

APPLE-BLOSSOM TABLECLOTH

Edging

I worked this pattern with Coats no. 20 Mercer crochet cotton wound on two shuttles, but any thread of similar thickness could be used. I have drawn little arrows on the chains in the flow diagram at the start of this pattern. Work alphabetically – two rings, chain, two rings, chain – and, apart from the ends of the rows, that is all there is to it! I don't think it really matters which shuttle you use for any individual ring; I used whichever was nearest, and this worked out quite neatly. As you will see, the corner is made by leaving out the edging trefoil on the footing side three times. Follow the arrows on the diagram to form the outer edge of the lace at the corner for

the beginning of the second side. Sew out at point G, and cut off the threads. Rejoin threads at point H, and follow the arrows on the chains to continue the second side.

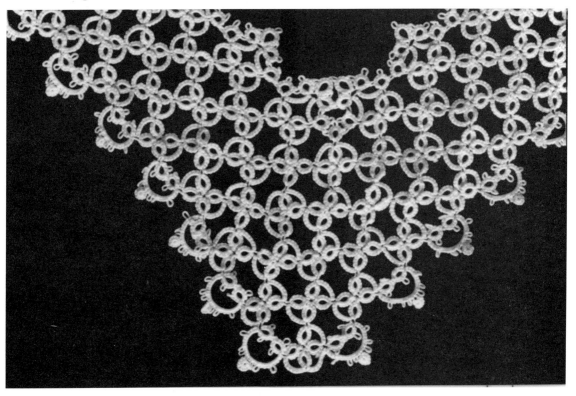

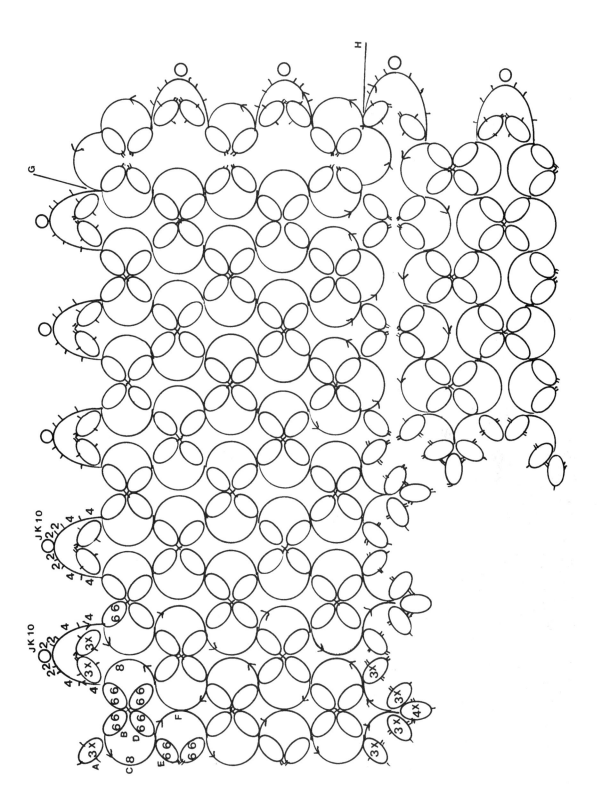

Insertion

This insertion has virtually the same pattern as the edging, but is worked in rounds, starting from the middle.

You need to be very careful when adding the insertion to the cloth – you will waste a lot of time hemstitching if you cut the cloth in the wrong place! Don't panic – just measure the distance from the edging very accurately, tack the tatting in place equally accurately, and buttonhole round it, catching in the picots as you come to them. Then, when you are absolutely sure, cut away the material from behind.

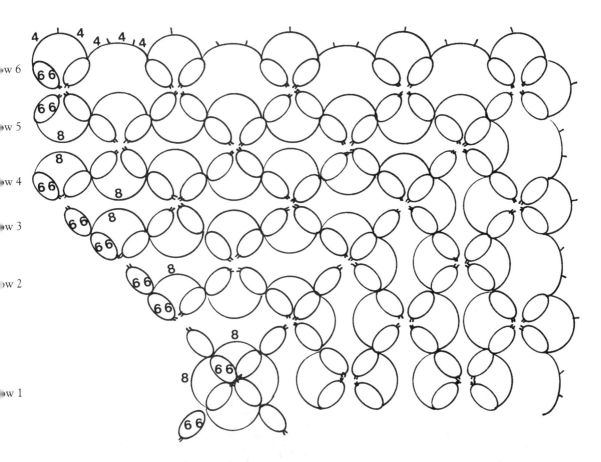

Row 6

Row 5

Row 4

Row 3

Row 2

Row 1

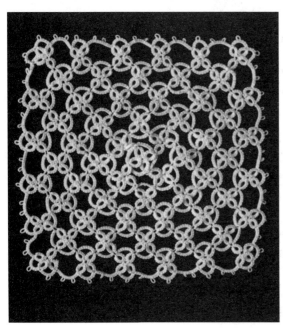

TEA-COSY INSERTION

If you have worked your way through the edging and insertion for the Apple-blossom tablecloth, you will not need any instructions for this!

If you don't want to make your own tea-cosy pad, I'm sure you could buy one and make a paper pattern for the cover simply by drawing round it and allowing for seams. Hemstitch along the bottom edge, then make up the cover and tack the insertion to the middle of one side, as far or as near to the hemstitching as pleases you. Buttonhole round it, as described for the insertion on p. 48.

Now get out your best silver teapot, and invite your friends to tea!

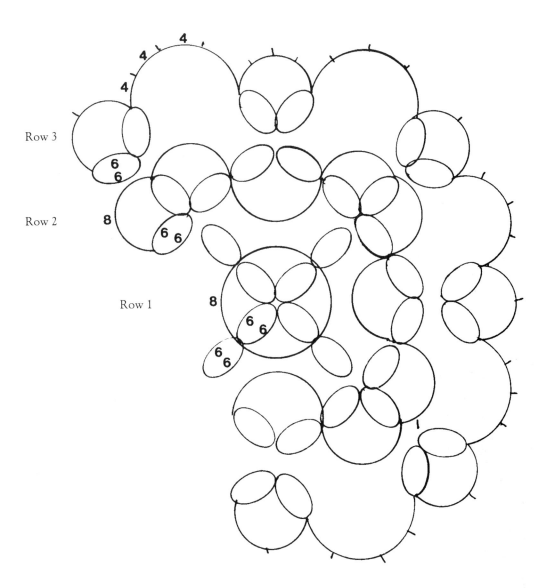

Row 3

Row 2

Row 1

SMALL TABLECLOTH

When I first made this edging, it was
intended to be a little table-napkin to go
with the Apple-blossom teacloth (p. 46–9).
However, I obviously didn't make this clear
to my brother and sister-in-law when I gave
it to them to photograph, and they used it
as a separate small mat. I really think they
were right, as it's too wide and heavy for a
teatime napkin. The ball thread could be
wound on to a second shuttle for the
Josephine knot, but when I was working it
I found myself using whichever shuttle was
nearest to the ring I was about to make. On
the whole, I think this gives a neater result.
I worked the whole set in no. 20 crochet
cotton.

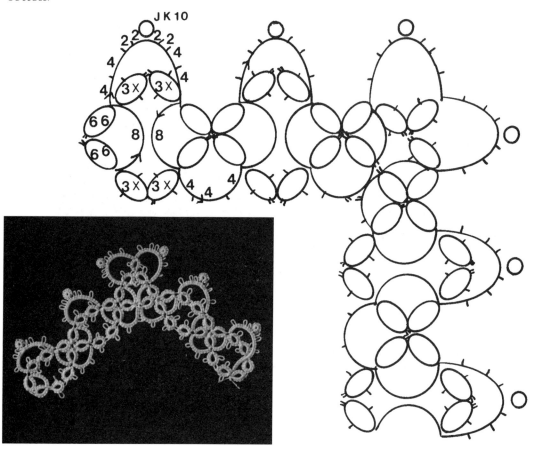

ITEMS FOR A
CRAFT STALL

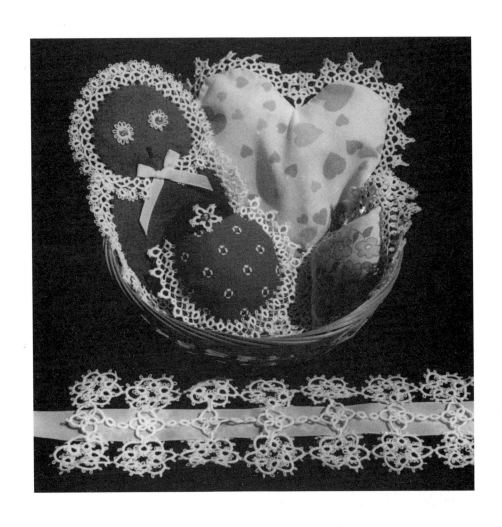

BABY OWL NEEDLECASE

Make a paper pattern for this by tracing around the outside line of fig. a and again around the inner line on the body for the 'pages' of the needlecase. Cut two pieces of felt from each pattern, making the owl brown and the pages white. Sew the pages on to the back half of the owl at the neck, and sew two eyes and a beak on to the front half. The eyes are rings of 12 ds, separated by 2 ds in no. 20 cotton and held in place by a gold spangle and a small gold bead. Attach the tatted edging to the front body section, then pin the two sections together round the head. Attach the tatted edging round the head, sewing through both thicknesses and finishing below the beak. Attach a bow of narrow ribbon over the join. The tatting is worked in no. 40 crochet cotton, wound on

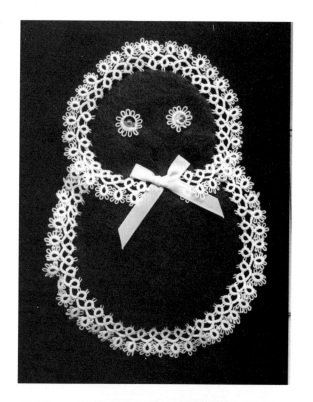

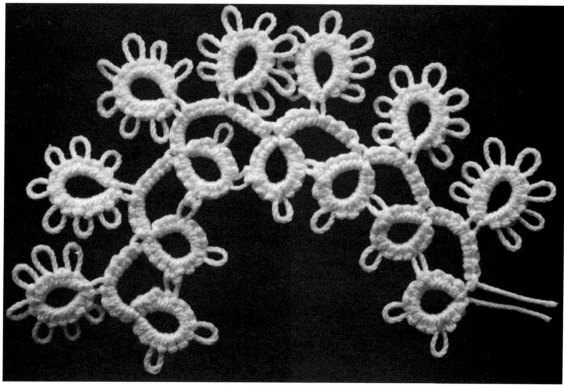

to two shuttles. (I have worked out a corner
for this design, though you will not need to
use it for the owl.)

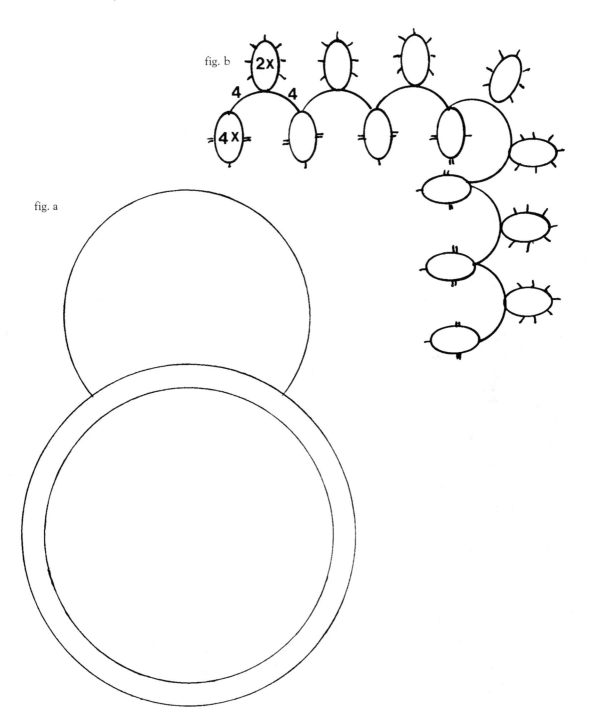

fig. b

fig. a

HEART-SHAPED LAVENDER BAG

Make the pattern for the heart by tracing over fig. a. Cut two pieces of thin muslin, sew them together and fill with dried lavender.

The tatting is straightforward. I used no. 40 DMC Cordonnet Special, and wound the ball thread on to a second shuttle to work the trefoil. The three picots on the central ring are worked consecutively. The reverse corner fits into the shape at the top of the heart, so ignore it if you want to use the edging for a handkerchief.

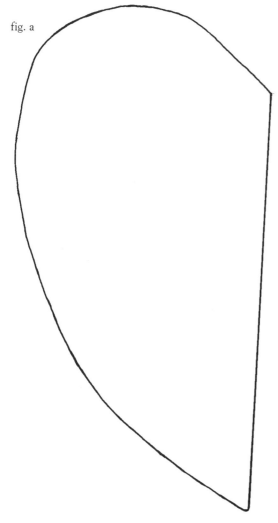

fig. a

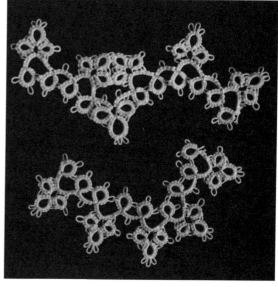

fig. b

A BRIDE'S GARTER

It is difficult to show this design clearly in a diagram; it needs a bit of explanation. It is worked in no. 40 crochet cotton, with the ball thread wound on to a second shuttle.

Ring 2 ds p nine times, 2 ds. First chain: 1 ds p, 4 ds p, 5 ds p, twice, 5 ds. *Ring, as above. Chain 5 ds p three times, 5 ds. Repeat from * until five rings and chains have been completed; join to first p on first chain. Chain 6 ds p (with the ridge, and thus the p, on the inside). Reverse work. Chain 6. Ring 8 ds p 8 ds. Chain 8 ds. Using second shuttle, ring 8 ds p 8 ds. Resume first shuttle. Chain 8 ds; ring 8 ds, join p (see diagram) 8 ds. Chain 6 ds, reverse work,

1 ds, p, 6 ds p. This gets you to the base of the lower flower, which is worked in the same way as the upper one, except that the p on the first chain is unnecessary, as you can complete the flower circle by joining it into the last p on the 6 ds chain.

Now complete the second half of the middle section, and end by joining to the p on the first chain. Care must be taken to do this *behind* the flower, so you can start the chain at the back, where the ribbon is held. The chain is worked (4 ds p, 4 ds p, 4 ds join p, reverse work) and repeated 10 times to reach the starting point on the next flower. When finished, thread with blue ribbon.

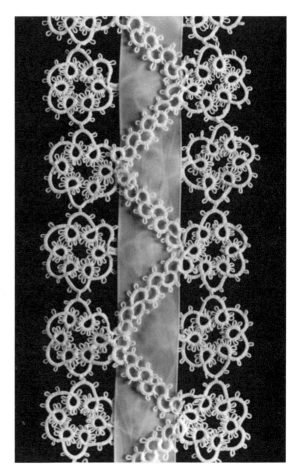

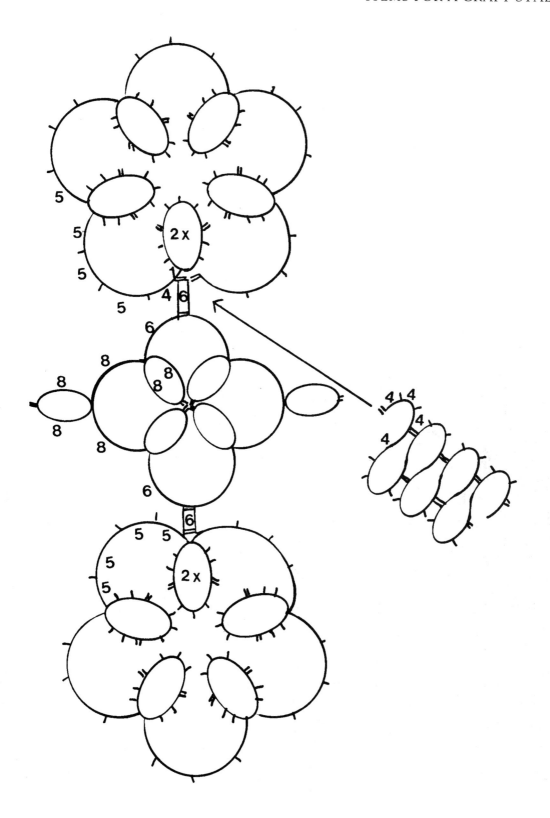

LADYBIRD PINCUSHION

Cut out a 15 cm. (6 in.) circle of red
material, preferably spotted. Gather it
round the edge, pull up thread and stuff
tightly. New (raw) wool is good for this,
because the lanolin in the wool stops the
pins rusting. Trace a pattern from fig. a and
cut it out in black felt for the head. Sew the
straight edges together to make a cone; stuff
and attach to the body (this forms the head).
Cut a small circle about 3 cm. across and
sew it over the gathers to neaten. The eyes
are small black beads.

You will need about 23–24 cm. of tatting
for the skirt (without the corner, of course).
The little hat is made from five repeats of
the large ring of the skirt edging, i.e. 4 ds p 6
ds 3 ps, 6 ds p 4 ds, worked close together

to form a circle. Attach to the head with a
spangle and a small gold bead.

fig. a

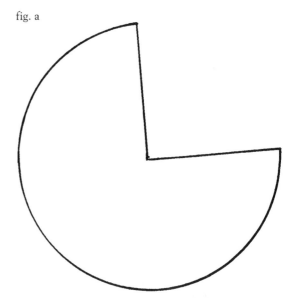

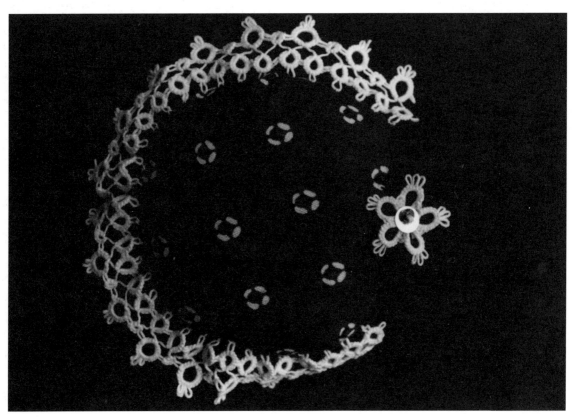

fig. b

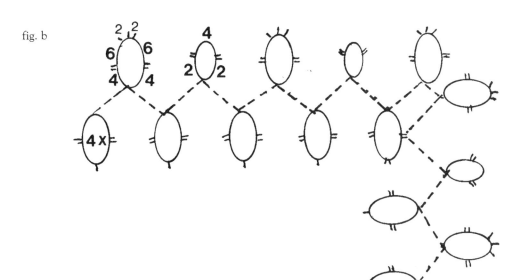

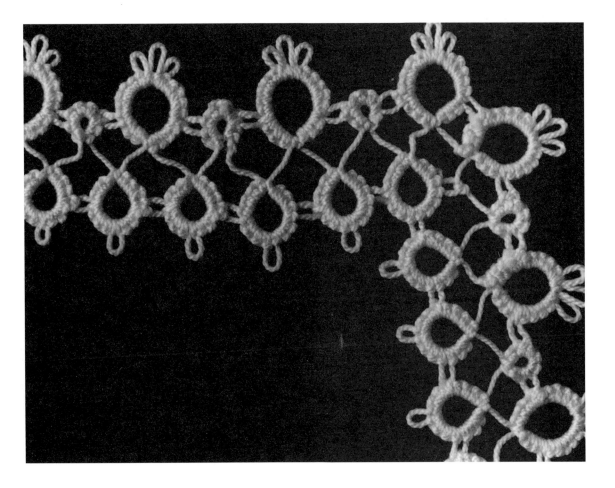

SQUARE PINCUSHION

Both rows of this pattern need the thread wound on two shuttles, in row 1 for the little horizontal ring in the middle of each repeat, and in row 2 for the 4 ds p 2 ds p 4 ds ring that joins it to the first row.

Don't worry about the variation in the lengths of the chains that appear on the drawing (at the corner, for instance). These are intended to make it easier for you to see where the rings join up. The size of your pincushion is entirely up to you. Mine is about 6 cm. (2½ in.) square, and the tatting is done in no. 40 cotton. When worked in a much finer thread, say 80 or 100, this pattern also looks nice on a handkerchief.

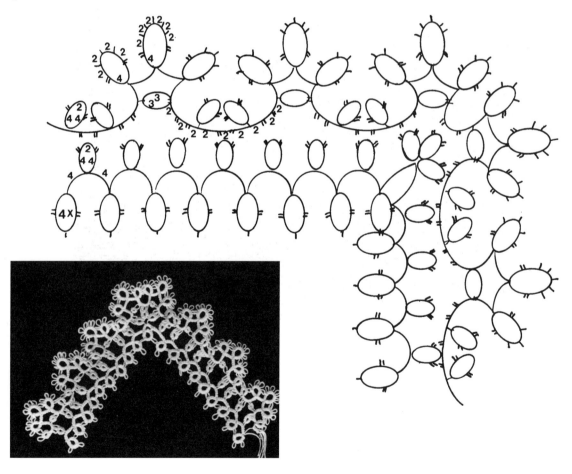

INSERTIONS

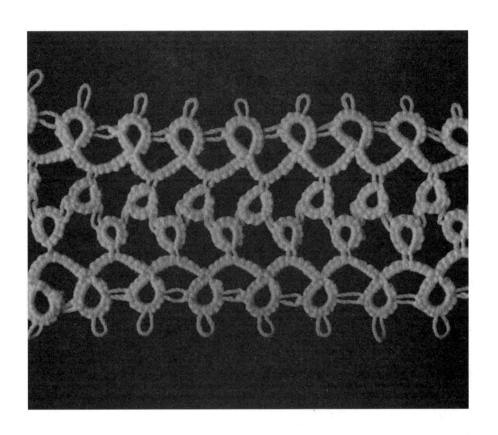

This project is the only one in the book that never got off the ground.

I happened to walk past a house where the lace curtains were not the usual machine-made nylon stuff you can buy by the yard, but wide strips of Torchon inserted into a fine muslin. They looked lovely, so I thought I could design something similar in tatting: a strip of flower-type circles, I decided, with a straight insertion on either side. The circles were easy enough, but I got a bit carried away with the insertions, made four, and could not make up my mind which I preferred. I therefore put them aside and got on with something else.

Then I moved house, and my new sitting-room had a window something over seven feet wide. I bought some plain muslin curtains to safeguard my privacy in the meantime, and somehow or other the tatting never got inserted.

So I give you all four, and you can make up your own mind which to use. I would suggest no. 20, or even no. 10 thread, according to the thickness of the muslin.

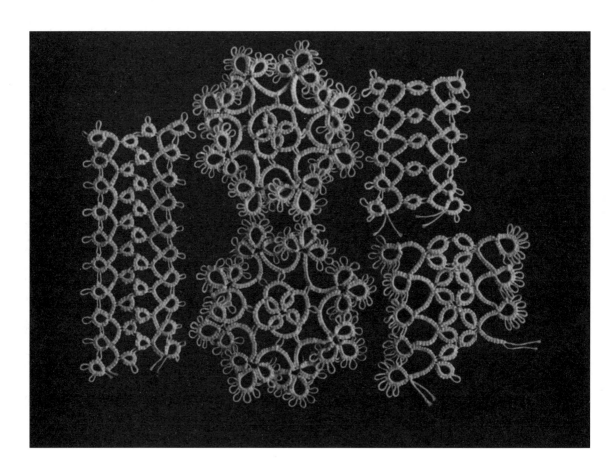

INSERTION A

This insertion is worked in two rows, the first having the ball thread wound on to a second shuttle to make the central row of rings. The second row, of course, simply picks up the p, as indicated in the diagram.

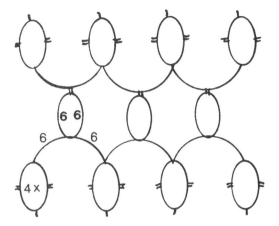

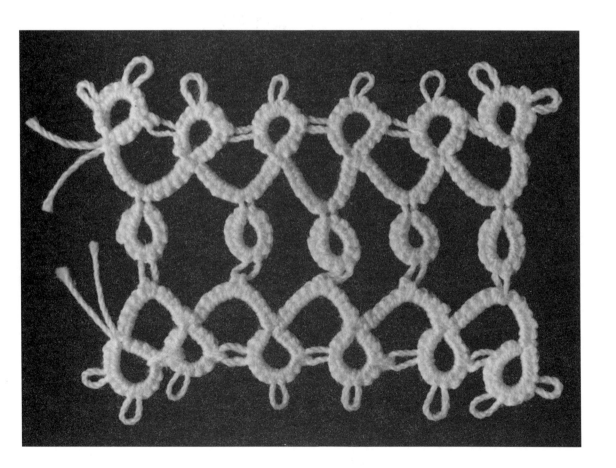

INSERTION B

This pattern is very similar to the previous design, only this time, both rows need the second shuttle to work the middle rings.

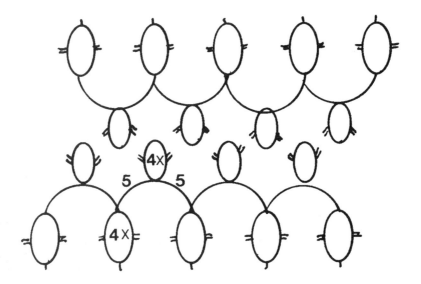

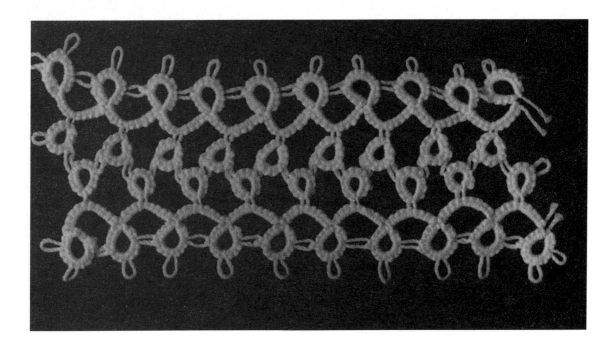

INSERTION C

This pattern is worked in two identical rows, joined in the middle to form a flower. The ball thread needs to be wound on to a second shuttle for these middle rings.

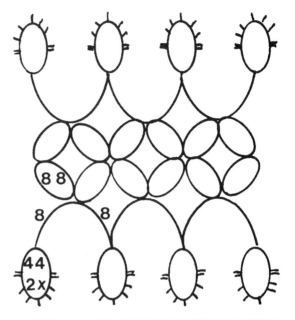

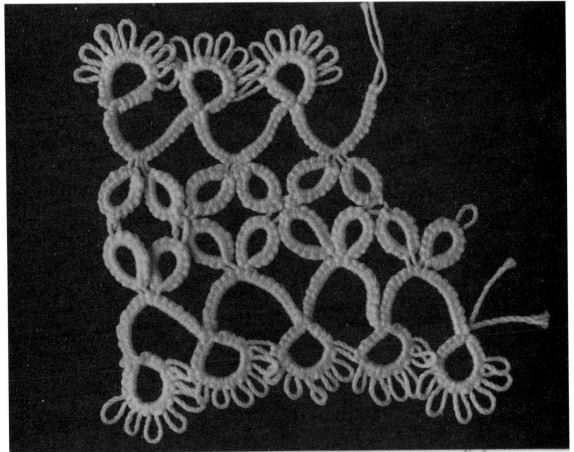

INSERTION D

This is a straightforward-enough pattern for an insertion for a lace curtain. Whether it would work equally well if the strips were joined side by side, I am not sure. I think there would be large gaps between them, and smaller circles would be necessary to fill these. Here is your chance to do a bit of experimenting!

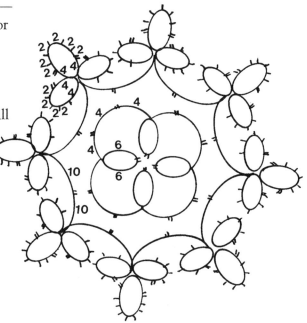

A YOKE

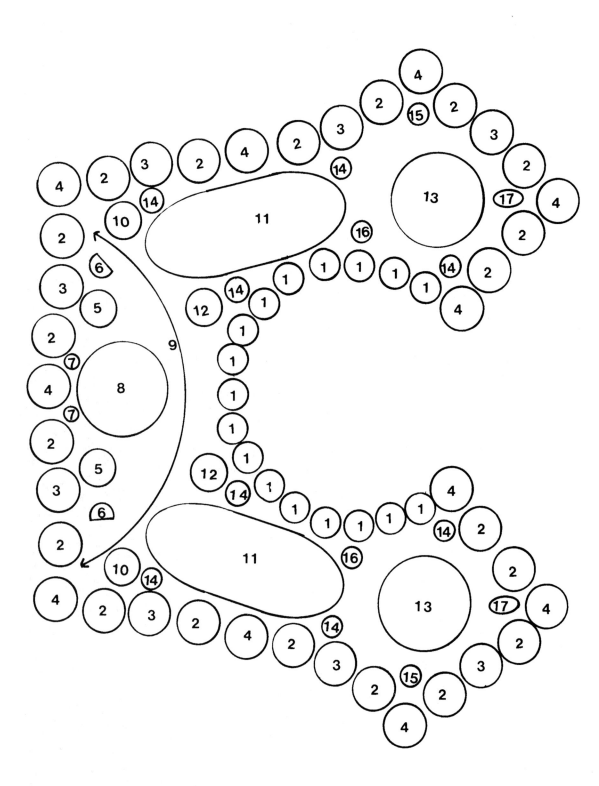

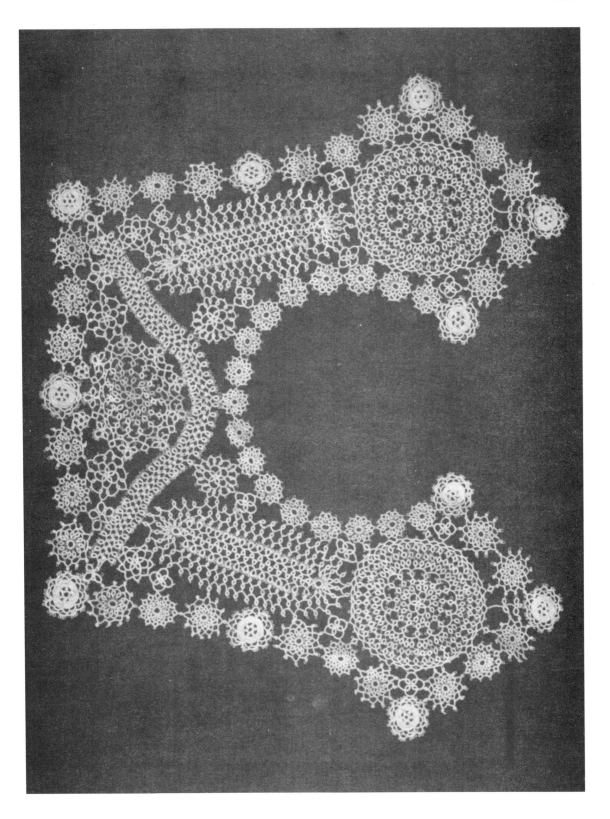

This yoke looks complicated, and in fact it was tricky to make for the first time, but I hope I have been able to smooth out the problems and that it is now simple to copy.

I imagined it on a dark-coloured, high-necked and long-sleeved evening dress. I started by cutting out the shape from a size-14 dress pattern. In this way I could tack the various parts to it, to make sure that it lay flat and that all the pieces fitted into one another.

There is no real significance in the numbering of the different motifs, and I cannot see that it matters in which order you do them. I started with the central circle at the front, and the long curved wreath over it, but it would probably be easiest to start with the front edging circles and then work the various patterns that join on to it.

I am assuming that by the time you get to this pattern you will be a sufficiently experienced tatter to be able to work out from the photographs exactly where each piece joins on to its neighbours. Do not forget that one side is a mirror image of the other, so if the photograph shows only, for instance, the left-hand view of a certain motif, the right-hand side will have its joins reversed. I don't think this will be difficult, and I would not want to insult your intelligence by describing individually every single join.

I have to admit I am really rather fond of this design, and do hope you enjoy working – and eventually wearing – it. I worked it in no. 50 crochet cotton; you could vary the size by increasing or decreasing the thickness of the cotton.

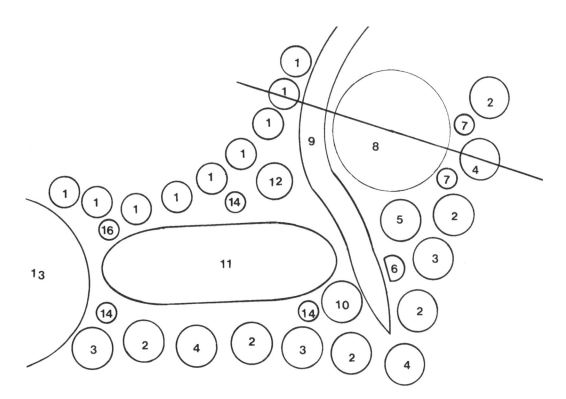

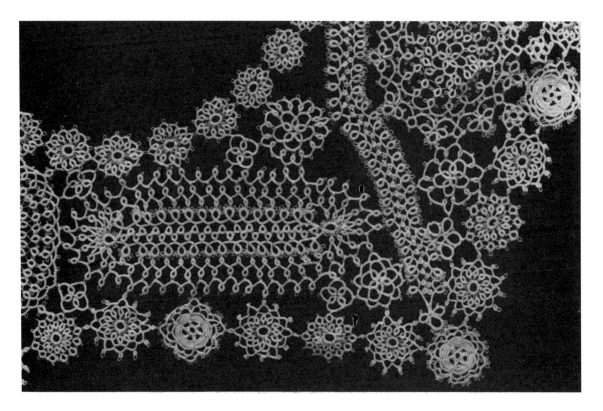

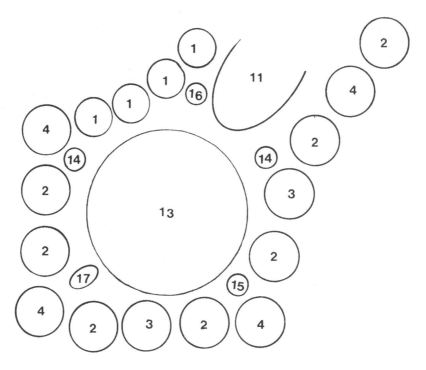

YOKE CIRCLE 1

First Row Ring, 1 ds p, then 2 ds p 11 times and close ring. Sew in ends.

Second Row Ring 6 ds, join to any p on first row, 6 ds, close. Chain 3 ds p 3 ds. Repeat all round.

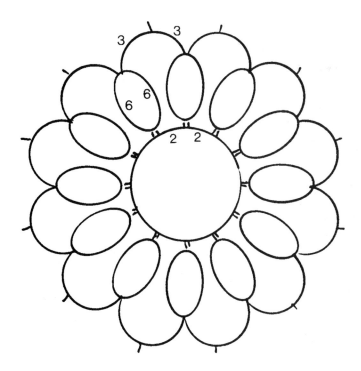

YOKE CIRCLE 2

The first two rows of this circle are the same as those in circle 1. The third row has to be worked with two shuttles, the first for the chain and the second for the small 3 ds p 3 ds rings.

YOKE CIRCLE 3

First row This is worked as for the two previous yoke circles.

    Second row R 6 ds, join to any p on row 1, 6 ds, close, leave about 3 mm. thread, R. 4 ds p three times, 4 ds. Repeat all round.

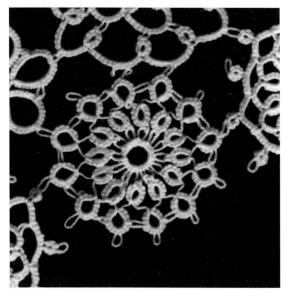

YOKE CIRCLE 4

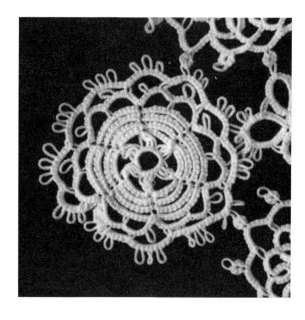

Row 1 R. 1 ds, 17 long p (about 4 mm.) separated by 1 ds, i.e. worked consecutively. Close ring and tie threads together to form 18th long p. Do not cut threads.

Row 2 Hook three long picots together with 1 ds. Chain 6 ds. Repeat all round. Again, do not cut threads.

Rows 3, 4 and 5 Chain 8, 10 and 6 ds p 6 ds respectively, joining shuttle thread to previous join.

Rows 6 and 7 As shown in the diagram.

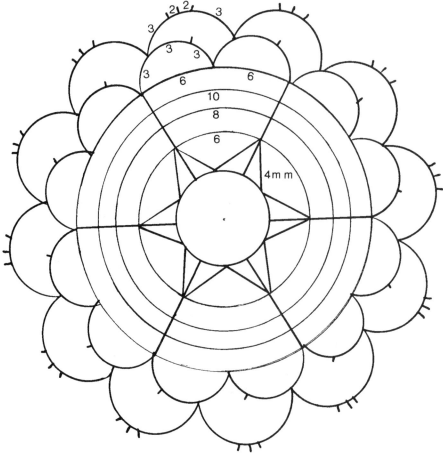

YOKE CIRCLE 5

This is simple enough, and can be followed from the diagram without further explanation.

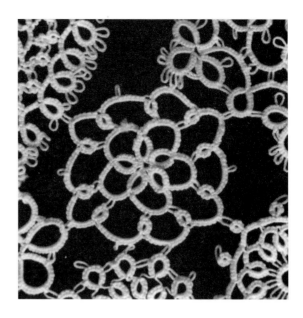

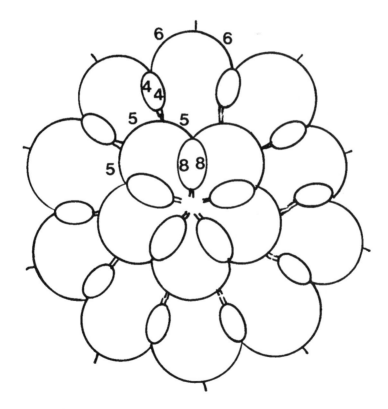

YOKE CIRCLE 6

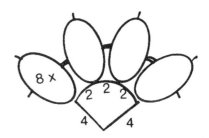

You will need two shuttles for this pattern. Leave the thread between them uncut so that you can hook it through the last p on the fifth ring and the first p of the sixth ring of the long garland (see p. 84 and photograph, p. 82). The chains are worked with shuttle 1 and the rings with shuttle 2.

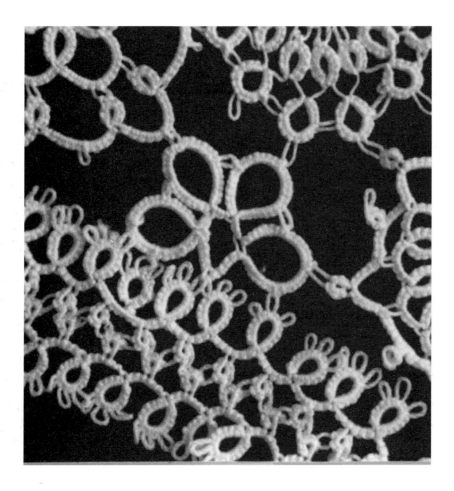

YOKE CIRCLE 7

Row 1 Ring 1 ds, 17 p (each p about 4 mm. long) separated by 1 ds, i.e. worked consecutively. Close ring and tie threads together to form 18th long p. Do not cut threads.

Row 2 Hook three long picots together with 1 ds. Chain 3 ds, p 3 ds. Repeat all round.

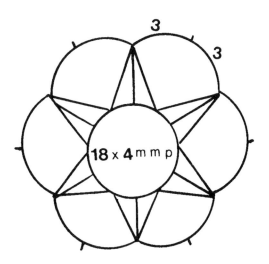

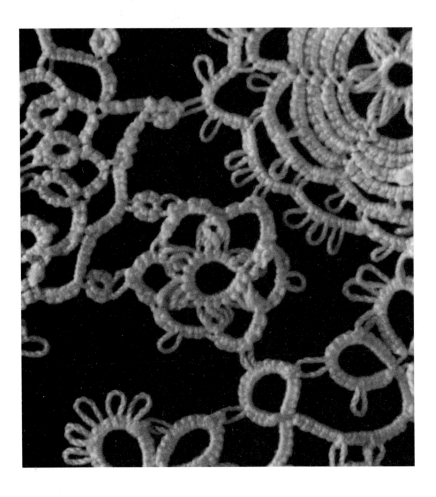

YOKE CIRCLE 8

I think this pattern is quite easy to follow
from the diagram, starting, obviously, with
the five rings forming the circle in the
middle, then working the five chains
between these, making three picots on each.
Because of this five-point start there is an
uneven number of trefoils on the outer ring.
When you come to fit this into its
surroundings, one of the trefoil groups goes at
the bottom to join on to circle 4, and one of
the intervening single rings goes at the top.
In this way the four trefoil groups can link up
with the garland (section 9, p. 84) as
illustrated.

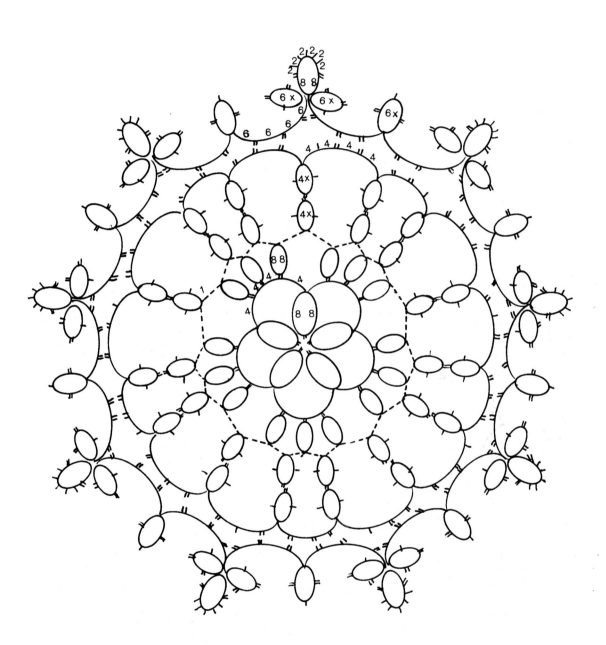

YOKE SECTION 9

This design needs two shuttles, one for the chains and trefoil, and the second for the small rings which interlink in the middle. The ends are illustrated in the photograph on this page, but the link-up with the large centre circle is best illustrated by the photograph on p. 82. There are 52 rings on the outer edge of this garland, and 53 on the inner edge, which attaches to circle 8 on the 18th, 24th, 30th and 36th rings from either end.

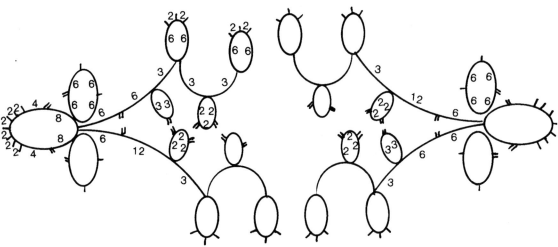

YOKE CIRCLE 10

This little circle is simple to work and is designed to link up the larger sections of the yoke. It is better left, therefore, until after you have worked sections 8, 9 and 11.

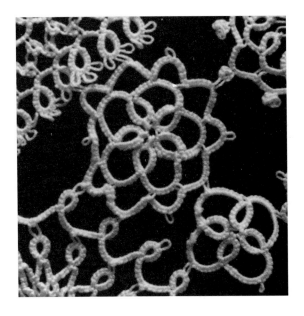

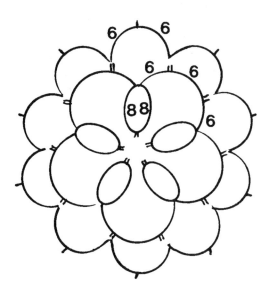

YOKE SECTION 11

The first row of this section is similar to that of the garland (section 9), requiring a second shuttle to work the small linking circles. However, here there is a large ring of 12 picots at the end, with 15 rings along each side. The rest of the section is easily followed from the diagram. The photograph shows the end in close-up; for the whole pattern, see p. 71.

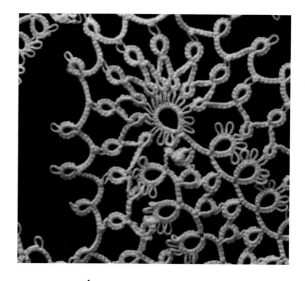

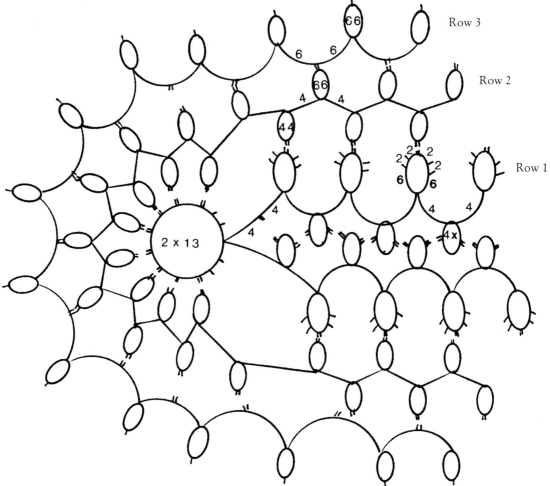

YOKE CIRCLE 12

No, this is not the same as circle 10 on p. 85! The space to be filled is a little larger, so the first chain has three picots instead of two.

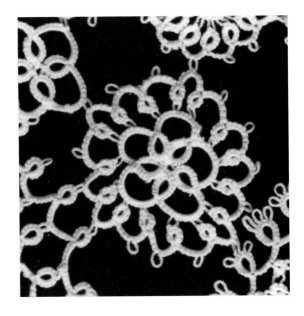

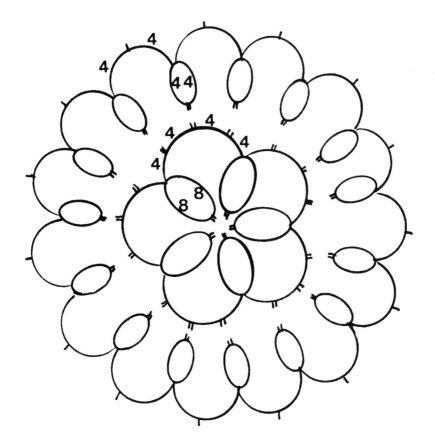

YOKE CIRCLE 13

I don't think you will have any difficulty
with this until you come to the sixth round.
You will need to wind the ball thread on to
a second shuttle to work the occasional
extra rings on the outside, which are
necessary to fill the odd spaces and which
link up with neighbouring rings. There are
five of these, and you can see from the
photograph where they occur. If this is not
specific enough, count the little 'tree' (yoke
circle 17) as one, and travel clockwise. The
rings occur on the 3rd, 12th, 18th, 28th and
44th chains.

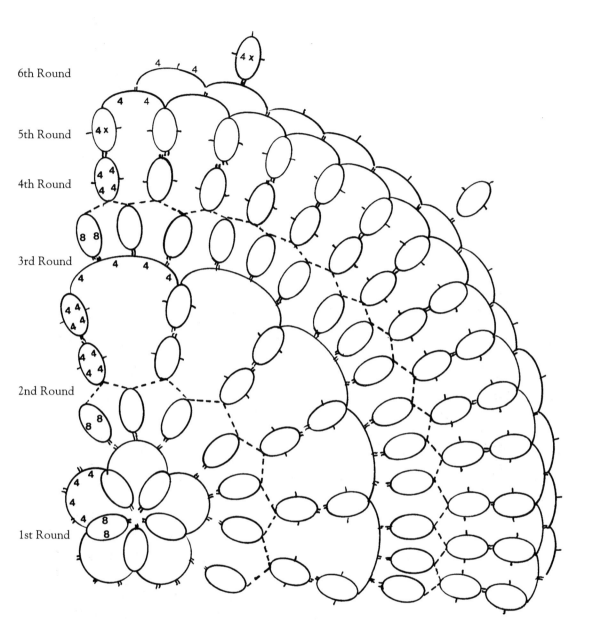

6th Round

5th Round

4th Round

3rd Round

2nd Round

1st Round

YOKE CIRCLES 14 AND 15

The small circles differ only slightly, in order to fit the spaces available, and their locations can be identified from the diagram on p. 70.

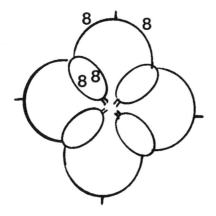

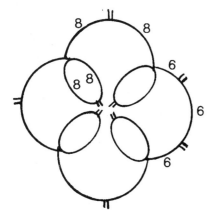

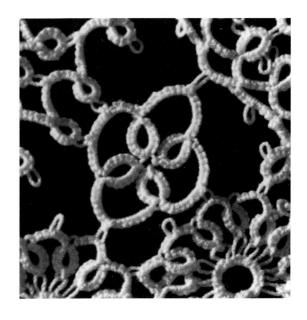

YOKE CIRCLE 16

This is another of the little filling-up circles, identifiable from the diagram on p. 70.

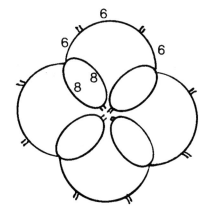

YOKE CIRCLE 17

This little 'tree' joins one of the corners to the large circle at the back of the yoke (see photograph on p. 88). Do not cut the thread between the ball and shuttle threads. You can hook this through the p on the large circle to commence the stalk.

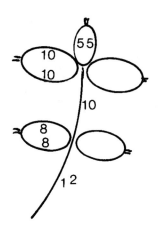

FURTHER READING

Books about Tatting

Cathy Bryant, *Tatting*, B.T. Batsford Ltd, 1992

Rebecca Jones, *The Complete Book of Tatting*, B.T. Batsford Ltd, 1985

Mary Konior, *A Pattern Book of Tatting*, B.T. Batsford Ltd, 1985

Tatting Patterns, Dryad Press, 1989

Tatting with Visual Patterns, B.T. Batsford Ltd, 1992

Other Useful Books

Gay Swift, *The Batsford Encyclopedia of Embroidery Techniques*, B.T. Batsford Ltd, 1984 (Contains instructions for hemstitching, mitreing corners, smocking, etc).

Jean Withers, *Mounting and Using Lace*, B.T. Batsford Ltd, 1986

BOOK SUPPLIERS

The following are stockists of the Batsford/Dryad Press range:

ENGLAND

AVON
Bridge Bookshop
7 Bridge Street
Bath BA2 4AS

Waterstone & Company
4–5 Milsom Street
Bath BA1 1DA

BEDFORDSHIRE
Arthur Sells
Lane Cover
49 Pedley Lane
Clifton
Shefford SG17 5QT

BUCKINGHAMSHIRE
J.S. Sear
Lacecraft Supplies
8 Hillview
Sherington MK16 9NJ

CAMBRIDGESHIRE
Dillons the Bookstore
Sidney Street
Cambridge

CHESHIRE
Lynn Turner
Church Meadow Crafts
7 Woodford Road
Winsford

DEVON
Creative Crafts & Needlework
18 High Street
Totnes TQ9 5NP

Honiton Lace Shop
44 High Street
Honiton EX14 8PJ

DORSET
F. Herring & Sons
27 High West Street
Dorchester DT1 1UP

Tim Parker *(mail order)*
124 Corhampton Road
Boscombe East
Bournemouth BH6 5NZ

Christopher Williams
19 Morrison Avenue
Parkstone
Poole BH17 4AD

DURHAM
Lacemaid
6, 10 & 15 Stoneybeck
Bishop Middleham DL17 9BL

GLOUCESTERSHIRE
Southgate Handicrafts
63 Southgate Street
Gloucester GL1 1TX

Waterstone & Company
89–90 The Promenade
Cheltenham GL50 1NB

HAMPSHIRE
Creative Crafts
11 The Square
Winchester SO23 9ES

Doreen Gill
14 Barnfield Road
Petersfield GU31 4DR

Needlestyle
24–26 West Street
Alresford

Ruskins
27 Bell Street
Romsey

ISLE OF WIGHT
Busy Bobbins
Unit 7
Scarrots Lane
Newport PO30 1JD

KENT
The Handicraft Shop
47 Northgate
Canterbury CT1 1BE

Denis Hornsby
25 Manwood Avenue
Canterbury CT2 7AH

LONDON
W. & G. Foyle Ltd
113–119 Charing Cross Road
WC2H 0EB

Hatchards
187 Piccadilly W1V 9DA

MIDDLESEX
Redburn Crafts
Squires Garden Centre
Halliford Road
Upper Halliford
Shepperton TW17 8RU

NORFOLK
Stitches and Lace
Alby Craft Centre
Cromer Road
Alby
Norwich NR11 7QE

Jane's Pincushions
Taverham Craft Unit 4
Taverham Nursery Centre
Fir Covert Road
Taverham
Norwich NR8 6HT

Waterstone & Company
30 London Street
Norwich NR2 1LD

NORTH YORKSHIRE
Craft Basics
9 Gillygate
York

Shireburn Lace
Finkle Court
Finkle Hill
Sherburn in Elmet LS25 6EB

The Craft House
23 Bar Street
Scarborough YO13 9QE

SOMERSET
Bridge Bookshop
62 Bridge Street
Taunton TA1 1UD

STAFFORDSHIRE
J. & J. Ford (*mail order & lace days only*)
October Hill
Upper Way
Upper Longdon
Rugeley WS15 1QB

SUSSEX
Waterstone & Company
120 Terminus Road
Eastbourne

WARWICKSHIRE
Christine & David Springett
21 Hillmorton Road
Rugby CV22 6DF

WEST MIDLANDS
Needlewoman
21 Needles Alley
off New Street
Birmingham B2 5AG

WEST YORKSHIRE
Sebalace
Waterloo Mill
Howden Road
Silsden BD20 0HA

George White Lacemaking Supplies
40 Heath Drive
Boston Spa LS23 6PB

Just Lace
Lacemaker Supplies
14 Ashwood Gardens
Gildersome
Leeds LS27 7AS

Jo Firth
58 Kent Crescent
Lowtown, Pudsey
Leeds LS28 9EB

WILTSHIRE
Everyman Bookshop
5 Bridge Street
Salisbury SP1 2ND

SCOTLAND

Embroidery Shop
51 William Street
Edinburgh
Lothian EH3 7LW

Waterstone & Company Ltd
236 Union Street
Aberdeen AB1 1TN

WALES

Bryncraft Bobbins (*mail order*)
B.J. Phillips
Pantglas
Cellan
Lampeter
Dyfed SA48 8JD

Hilkar Lace Suppliers
33 Mysydd Road
Landore
Swansea

EQUIPMENT SUPPLIERS

ENGLAND

See also pp. 93–5

BERKSHIRE
Chrisken Bobbins
26 Cedar Drive
Kingsclere RG15 8TD

CAMBRIDGESHIRE
Josie and Jeff Harrison
Walnut Cottage
Winwick
Huntingdon PE17 5PP

ESSEX
Needlework
Ann Bartleet
Bucklers Farm
Coggeshall CO6 1SB

GLOUCESTERSHIRE
Chosen Crafts Centre
46 Winchcombe Street
Cheltenham GL52 2ND

NORTH HUMBERSIDE
Teazle Embroideries
35 Boothferry Road
Hull

SURREY
Needlestyle
5 The Woolmead
Farnham GU9 7TX

SUSSEX
Southern Handicrafts
20 Kensington Gardens
Brighton BN1 4AC

WEST MIDLANDS
Framecraft
83 Hampstead Road
Handsworth Wood
Birmingham B2 1JA

SCOTLAND

Christine Riley
53 Barclay Street
Stonehaven

Peter and Beverley Scarlett
Strupak
Hill Head
Cold Wells, Ellon
Grampian

RING OF TATTERS

Miss B. Netherwood
269 Oregon Way
Chaddesden
Derby DE2 6UR